What People are Saying About BIG GOALS...Short Deadlines

Mickey Straub has done things that a lot of us have only dreamed of and has outlined his strategy for success for you in *BIG GOALS...Short Deadlines.* Twenty years ago, I met this guy in the gym and now Mickey is a good friend and my mayor. I'm in his corner!

Bo Jackson
Former 2 Sport All-Star
President/CEO, VEJ Holdings LLC

* * * * *

BIG GOALS...Short Deadlines is a must-read. Learn from it and put it into action in your own life. The book showcases what you can do, if and when you put your mind to something, regardless of the degree of difficulty. To see 50 capitols in 50 days is remarkable because of the enormous time investment and intricate logistics. Not only did he accomplish this, but the findings he uncovered were remarkable.

I coach champions for a living and Mickey Straub is the epitome of a champion. His unwavering self-discipline, concentration, optimism, relaxation, and enjoyment regarding this trip and the writing of this book are Zone worthy. Read his book and leverage his wisdom and knowledge.

Jim Fannin
America's ZoneCoach®

* * * * *

BIG GOALS...Short Deadlines is one of those books that truly captures "IT ALL."

Told in an easy-to-read story of one man's journey, the lessons on setting goals, forming habits, priority management, establishing values and obtaining results come shining through. It is rare when such large and complex topics as goals, country, spirituality and patriotism can all bleed harmoniously into one.

Mickey is a dear friend with great wisdom, great heart, and a great story. All who read this book will benefit in their career and life.

Edward Deutschlander, CLU, CLF
CEO, North Star Resource Group

★ ★ ★ ★ ★

What makes this so incredible is that Mickey Straub did not just travel to 50 capitol buildings in (less than) 50 days, he laid out his plan according to the foundation of his deeply-held philosophical and faith values. Certainly, he is the only person in history to deliver and contemplate Lincoln's Gettysburg Address in all 50 capitol buildings.

As such, we should give his advice consideration because there is no other person with the wisdom of his perspective.

John D. Morris
Director, Ronald W. Reagan Society of Eureka College

★ ★ ★ ★ ★

Mickey Straub masterfully sets goals and manages the activity required to accomplish them. By sharing his adventures through the 50 Capitols in 50 Days trip, he has given us a front row seat to his success and the perspective necessary for personal growth and accomplishments. His exceptional understanding of how people learn and apply knowledge transcends industries. Thank you, Mickey, for sharing your wisdom and experiences with us in *BIG GOALS...Short Deadlines.*

Daralee Barbera, CFP, CMFC, CLF, ChFC
Managing Principal, Waddell and Reed
GAMA International President 2014-2015

★ ★ ★ ★ ★

"You can get there from here" might be a proper paraphrase for the philosophy of author, mayor, businessman, and patriot Mickey Straub.

His new book *BIG GOALS…Short Deadlines* is a road map, not just of his physical journey to 50 state capitols in 50 days, but to positivity and the process of the goal planning and visualization that made it possible. I recommend this book to anyone who has a dream or a burning goal and needs some well-experienced tips on how to move forward.

Jim Peterik
Grammy-winning songwriter of the #1 motivational anthem of our time: "Eye of The Tiger"

★ ★ ★ ★ ★

During his 50 Capitols in 50 Days, Mickey has applied the same tools and philosophy he had been using the past two decades to help financial professionals accomplish their goals. His inspiring journey is a practical application of the tools, habits, measurement, and focus needed to achieve your goals and dreams. This book is a must read and the missing link to execution!

Joey Davenport
President, Hoopis Performance Network

★ ★ ★ ★ ★

If you want to tap into your full potential and start really achieving what you are capable of in your life, then you must read this book. Mickey has cracked the code of what it takes to get you to play your "A" game on a consistent basis.

Machen MacDonald
#1 Bestselling Author, Provoking Your Brilliance
Founder ProBrilliance Leadership Institute

★ ★ ★ ★ ★

Mickey Straub has written a good book on how to accomplish big goals and short deadlines with a patriotic and spiritual message. Read the book carefully and you will gain insight into some of the success strategies needed to achieve your goals. Remember to "measure and monitor what matters most."

Garry D. Kinder
Chief Executive Officer, Kinder Brothers International

★ ★ ★ ★ ★

Mickey's personal journey of 50 Capitols in 50 Days provides an example of what is possible when you follow your heart. In this book, Mickey offers a glimpse of the possible and attainable if you apply certain disciplines.

Jon R. O'Neal, CLU, LUTCF
Chartered Financial Consultant

★ ★ ★ ★ ★

This book is exactly what more Americans need today: good common sense ideas they can use.

Steven J. Fedewa
Vice President, Knights of Columbus

★ ★ ★ ★ ★

Debbie, Continued success and Blessings! [illegible] 5/4/16

BIG GOALS SHORT DEADLINES

MICKEY STRAUB

SAM, Inc.
Burr Ridge, Illinois

Published by SAM, Inc.
Burr Ridge, IL
www.SAMusa.com

Book design by TLC Graphics, *www.TLCGraphics.com*
Cover: Tamara Dever, Interior: Erin Stark

The Holy Bible, King James Version. Cambridge Edition: 1769;
King James Bible Online, 2015. *www.kingjamesbibleonline.org*.

Proudly printed in the United States of America

Library of Congress number: 2015920281

ISBN: 978-0-9970131-7-7

Table of Contents

Preface

"It is the homestretch, not of a ball game, but of a trip. If you are not *a sports enthusiast or a traveler, you may want to consider it the end of an intense project or the near-completion of a mammoth goal. In my case, for me, it has to do with a trip, an incredible trip, many others, including myself, thought may be unachievable. It has been an amazing trip that has brought out the best in people, especially in me; I have seen it firsthand. It has also been humbling, extremely humbling.*

When I woke up this morning, I had the usual thoughts: Can I still succeed? Where am I? How far is there to go? What do I have to do today? How many hours of sleep have I had? And, the big ones, "Will I have the energy to finish?" and "Will it really matter?"

Those words were written by me when I was in Coeur d'Alene, Idaho, while sitting on a couch early that foggy morning looking out over that magnificent lake by the same name. It was day 39, with 44 capitols behind me. I continued:

"It's undeniable that this stretch, this calling up every ounce of energy, power, and fortitude that I can muster,

> *is making a difference for me and on me. But the real hope that I have, the real driving force for this trip, this metaphor in life, is that it will make a difference in other people's lives. That gives me energy. Sure, I can do things to make me happy and that will get me going. But the real excitement that I get is from making other people happy or the feeling that I am making a difference in other peoples' lives."*

It was never my intention to write a book on how I was able to achieve my goal of visiting 50 capitols in 50 days. But the realization that the very strategies and techniques that were used to build our company and serve our clients for many years were the same strategies and techniques I needed to succeed on this journey. It was an accidental, yet life-changing discovery!

It was day two in Vermont when it hit me that if I was not extremely disciplined and organized, more disciplined than I had been in years or perhaps in my lifetime, then I was going to fail! Then came the realization, the honest reflection of my recent past, that I had been undisciplined for a long time. It hit me like a ton of bricks! Boy, that was a tough pill to swallow...to admit that I was off course and a bit of a hypocrite, maybe even lazy! But it was a truth that I had to reckon with, and I knew at that moment that I was in trouble.

This was a humbling awakening: I had fallen off-track myself and gotten into some bad habits. I needed to change ASAP and start practicing what I had been preaching or else I would FAIL! I needed to employ the very habits and determination that I had used to build a business and maintain solid and trusted relationships with clients, or the trip would be sunk and all of my efforts and those of others who helped in this initiative would be wasted. This was an unexpected discovery.

This book was never part of the initial plan. It didn't even enter my thoughts until I serendipitously ended up at the breakfast table overlooking scenic Lake Coeur d'Alene at the home of my wife's college friend whose family happened to be on vacation in Washington State. On my way across the Northwest, we contacted them and they were kind enough to give me their garage code to get into their house just hours before I arrived. It, like so many other things on the trip, just fell into place.

The words just started coming that day and so did the dream of a book, which percolated for a couple of years. I just knew that I had to share the discovery, however accidental, of the formula for success on my crazy journey. This formula for success helped me overcome thoughts of quitting countless times.

My historic trip to 50 capitols in 50 days proved to me that an effective goal-achievement strategy does exist… and that it can help anyone achieve their goals both large and small! It was like a discovery of a hidden treasure that had been under my feet for years that could help people maximize results, minimize regrets, and get more done in less time. After I returned from my trip, this same strategy helped me achieve a lifelong dream of being elected to public office as mayor of a Chicago suburb. I won the election against all the odds and predictions. It has been an honor to serve the people of my village and it's a privilege to have the opportunity to learn and make a difference.

This book is not about a trip nor is it about an election. Or maybe it is. Maybe it's about *your trip* through life and *your campaign* to realize your potential? It is about the lessons I learned along the way that can be applied to help you accomplish any goal, personal or professional, big or small. Fellow Baby Boomers, this book can help you get one step closer to crossing the items off your bucket list. Don't write them off as impossible! If I can overcome insurmountable odds and internal pessimism to make a dream come to fruition, then so can you!

I am excited that you chose to read *BIG GOALS…Short Deadlines: Success Strategies Inspired by One Man's Trip to 50 Capitols in 50 Days*. It's not just about a trip around the country; it's a road map of a different kind. Now, you get to share in this treasure of personal discovery and uncover the opportunities and life experiences that are all around you!

It was an accidental discovery, but success is not an accident.

To your success,

Mickey Straub

Acknowledgments

Much of the writing of BIG GOALS...Short Deadlines was done at various Starbucks locations in and around Burr Ridge, especially Western Springs, Clarendon Hills, Oak Brook, and Hinsdale, Illinois; though I also made progress at stores out of town, too, like in Lake Geneva and Milwaukee. There's just something about the energy and music of the communal atmosphere and the shared values that I felt from fellow patrons that sparked my creativity and gave me inspiration. Thank you Starbucks!

I also made numerous excursions to two other locations to find privacy and collect my thoughts. My deep gratitude goes out to John Morris, Director of the Ronald W. Reagan Society at Eureka College (Eureka, IL) where I would camp out for a couple of days in their old Presidential Guest House, as well as to Father Tom Koys of St. James Church at Sag Bridge (Lemont, IL) who allowed me to frequently use the rectory for some spiritual uplifting. As a way of showing my eternal gratitude, these two organizations will share in part of the proceeds from the sale of this book.

Let me start out with saying thank you again to my friends and family who bookended this journey, with special thanks to Jim Long, Sheri Lessig, Chris Faron, and Dick Coan. They were so deeply involved with the planning and execution of the plan, that I doubt either the trip or the book would have been possible without their help.

Some needed encouragement to tell the story after the trip was over was also received from some unsuspecting places. I am so thankful to the preceding mayor of Burr Ridge, Gary Grasso, and my pastor, Father William DeSalvo of St. Isaac Jogues Church and Mike Ellis of Hinsdale Magazine whose enthusiasm helped fuel my own to memorialize the trip and the lessons learned along the way. A year later, I also serendipitously met Emmy Award Winner and author, Glen Aubrey, at the 150th Anniversary of the Gettysburg Address, who encouraged me to write multiple books on the trip and lessons learned. (We are also kindred spirits; Glen has written several books about our 16th President and leadership.)

Thank you also to my good friend and best-selling author Machen MacDonald for his coaching along my writing journey and for ultimately connecting me with the publishing team. From the moment that I went to Tamara Dever's company website for TLC Graphics, I felt like I had come home. She has been a blessing, as have her colleagues, Heidi Sheard and Erin Stark, who edited and formatted every page and made this dream become a reality.

I would also be remiss if I failed to mention my inner circle who I entrusted to give an honest appraisal and candid feedback of the first completed manuscript. Thank you to my two sisters and one of my brothers, Ginny Hahn, Jolly Koebele, and Joe Straub, as well as Matt Baron, Jim Fannin and Tom O'Brien, who helped to make *BIG GOALS... Short Deadlines* the best it can be. I would also like to thank my dear friends Steve Fedewa (Knights of Columbus), Art Heiman (AIG), and Jon O'Neal (American National) for the role they played in the trip and in encouraging me to write about the role that activity management can play in goal achievement.

No words can sufficiently express my love for my wife, Charmaine, and my appreciation to company staff for the countless times they all allowed me the time and flexibility to go and write this book. Their support and understanding made it possible for me to invest the time and effort to process, document, write, hone, and re-write what is contained within. There was just something that told us all that these lessons had to be shared.

There were so many people who told me during the trip, "God has His hands on you." Well, it appears that He still does. Thank you, Lord, for making this all possible. As I reflect on this life-changing trip done for love of God and country, I am deeply grateful to all the people who I met along the way to make this journey possible and for all the unsung heroes.

I would like to give special thanks to my sister, Jolly, and dedicate this book to her. She has always been my biggest cheerleader. I still have the picture that she sent to me back in college with the image of the Norman Rockwell painting of the little girl with a black eye outside of the principal's office with the caption, "I'll be there to cheer for you." During the 50 Capitols trip, I spoke with her virtually every night and doubt that I could have gotten through it without her daily encouragement and caring spirit which she shared even while in the midst of her own personal and financial challenges. It is no surprise that my sister's birth name is really "Mary" Jolly, considering the joy and selflessness she exudes, even in the face of adversity. Jolly, your selfless nature never ceases to amaze and humble me.

CHAPTER ONE

The Journey Begins

★ ★ ★ ★ ★ ★

As Americans, we are encouraged to dream from the moment we are born. From movies to television shows to commercials, it's as if we are being trained to dream. We grow up reading about dreams in childhood books, hearing about dreams in school, and seeing examples of dreams in movies: simply click your heels, wave a magic wand, or don a superhero costume and *voila*... your dreams can come true!

Our country itself is a classic example of a success story and an unlikely one at that. Built by men and women who had little more than "a dream of freedom and independence," our forefathers fended off the superior arms of their enemies and beat the odds in order to build the foundation for what Abraham Lincoln called, "The Last Best Hope of Earth." Dreaming is part of the fabric of our nation.

Have you ever dreamed of success or wondered if a secret to success really exists? Is there a key or combination that, once discovered, could virtually guarantee that the opening of the floodgates of prosperity would flow into your lap? How about a formula for success or a series of steps that, if followed, could assure your success in achieving any personal or career goal, New Year's Resolution, or something on your bucket list? I would be surprised if you did not.

For me, I have wondered and sought out the secrets of success since childhood. That was, perhaps, a bit of luck because what I learned during my formative years would form the foundation for what I would attempt in my fifties. Known to many as America's Zone Coach, Jim Fannin said this about my trip, "The 50 Capitols in 50 Days trip was a 'daunting task' that most human beings would not undertake!" And that it was.

Dreaming about it for years, I made every excuse for why it wasn't the right time, whether it was personnel issues, cash flow, or the potential $20,000 expense. Once launched, I thought about the pressures back at the office constantly, and I tried to manage from afar while fighting back fatigue. I questioned myself almost daily, especially in the mornings when I woke up exhausted in a strange bed, in a strange town wondering if I had the strength and resolve to carry on. It was the toughest thing that I have ever tried to accomplish physically, financially, and emotionally!

Looking back, the preparation for the trip didn't just start three months before the trip, but long before that. As I mentioned to a good friend and noted in my journal shortly before departure, "I feel like I have been training for this for years."

Searching for the keys to success and reading "How to" books was a part of my life even as a teenager thanks to my brother, Joe. Memorizing quotes from my parents had a profound impact on me as a kid, many of them I repeat to this day. Looking for the best, most efficient way to do something always made sense to me. With five older brothers and sisters, all of whom had been a mentor and hero to me at one time or another, I recognized from a young age the benefits of learning from the experiences of others, from those who have already been down the path that I was seeking.

When my business fell off-track early in my career (while in my thirties) and after a few other wake-up calls, I had two choices: to give up and accept it or to go out and seek the answers from people who have already been down this path. I chose the latter. What I set out to find were the secrets to success. What I also needed was the confidence to know that when I found them, that they would be effective for me!

My original motivation to find success in my career was pretty selfish in nature; I needed to turn my business around. I was fueled by optimism and personal drive. But, then came some external motivation when one day, I opened up the "Frequently Called Numbers" page in my phone directory and noticed that eighteen out of twenty names had been "whited out" and written over. Ninety percent of my closest and most trusted colleagues were gone from the company! Using a quote from the Apollo 13 Space Mission, I thought to myself, *Houston, we have a problem!* (For you young guys, you may need to Google

"Wite-out," the Bic brand correction fluid or white paste applied to paper to mask written or typographical errors.)

After talking with one of the newer sales reps, Vinnie, I learned that I was not the only one who had sought help from management and hit similar road blocks. My goal to find the best practices that could help my peers build their businesses intensified. We needed to figure out a way to increase productivity and lower the astoundingly high turnover of 85 percent in the first four years of someone's career in our industry-at-large. Then, my focus widened to include managers because while some may succeed alone, most will fail alone and nothing takes the place of good leadership.

Knowing that success leaves clues, I sought out and researched the most successful people that I could find, study, meet, or read about. I became a voracious reader and studied many of the greatest writers in the last century, like Og Mandino, who wrote seven inspirational books including two of my favorites: *The Greatest Salesman in the World* and *The Spellbinder's Gift*. I read books like Stephen Covey's, *7 Habits of Highly Effective People* and *Principled Centered Leadership*. I re-read several others including *Think and Grow Rich* by Napoleon Hill, *The Strangest Secret* by Earl Nightingale, and *How to Win Friends and Influence People* by Dale Carnegie.

I found nuggets of wisdom in so many books, parables, conversations, and even in articles like the one about singer John "Cougar" Mellencamp who was going through a bit of a metamorphosis of his own. In an attempt to grow up a little (my words), he chose to drop his middle nickname that reflected his younger, wild side (my words). The thing that really stuck with me was that he committed himself to a "lifelong self-improvement course." I liked Mellencamp's philosophy so much that I decided to adopt that phrase for myself. I was embarking on a journey of lifelong improvement.

Becoming a distributor for Nightingale/Conant Corporation, the pioneer in self-help audiotapes, I turned my car into a "university-on-wheels" to learn as much as I could, as fast as I could. It helped that, as a salesman who was on the road a lot, driving 30-40,000 miles per year, I had plenty of time to listen, learn, and reflect.

CHAPTER TWO

Time Management is a Misnomer

★ ★ ★ ★ ★ ★

During my search for the keys to success, I spent long hours researching, listening, studying, and attending seminars. There was one thing that came to the surface repeatedly and I suspected it could have a big impact on my business and in my career: *If I could just manage my TIME better... I would be more successful!*

When you think about it, we all have the same amount of time: 24 hours per day, 7 days per week, 12 months and 365 days or 8,760 hours of time every year to seek our goals and do whatever we wish. Some people seem to flourish while others flounder! *Why is that?* And though the same thing could be said for virtually any profession, in my world of sales, the disparity in income was huge with some earning five to ten times more based on the same amount of time and what appeared to be similar effort.

I became convinced that the key to success, both mine and others, had to do with how well each of us managed time, so learning how to better manage my time became my top priority. I studied practically every one of the latest time management tools available in those days like Day-Timer,

Day Runner, TIME Systems, Priority Manager, Franklin-Planner, and others. I considered myself a student of time management, while I'm sure my close friends and family thought of me as a time management junkie! Luckily "time management" was the big rage those days and that enabled me to read, study, attend seminars, and quiz many of the users of the various products on the market.

Day-Timer was the first time management system that I started using in my career. The fact that the manufacturer was headquartered in my birth state of Pennsylvania helped me feel a special kinship to the product. I welcomed being reminded of friends and family, but kept my eyes open for other alternatives. After a year or so, my sister, Ginny, introduced me to the FranklinPlanner which her company had just implemented. After Stephen Covey joined forces with them to become FranklinCovey, it really catapulted them ahead of their competitors at the time, so I tried their planner. The company grew quickly and even made substantial investments in case studies, training and research, and development of time management software which was just starting to become more widely accepted in the sales industry. I always remembered the results of one of their studies on this subject which I was told concluded that there was a better connection between the mind and the pencil, than the mind and the computer.

My journey of researching and trying various time management products continued. After a sales call one day, I accidentally ran across another product called TIME Systems. I attended their seminar, which helped me learn even more about establishing disciplined systems and managing the sales pipeline which were paramount to increasing business and ideas that I would use later in my career. All of this, of course, was done in an effort to control this thing called *time*!

After all that research, testing, and piloting of multiple time management programs over a period of years, I had two major revelations that changed my outlook forever. Here is the first one:

You Cannot...Manage Time!

You might be thinking, *Are you crazy? Sure you can...I have been managing my time all my life!* Time management courses have been taught for years. Countless books have been written on the subject of time management. They are household words and yet seems allusive to nearly everyone. Am I saying that you cannot manage time?

Actually, yes, that is exactly what I'm saying. You cannot manage time! Just try it. Is there anything you can do to speed up or slow down the hands of time? No. Can you save it up, store it, or trade it with anyone? No. Can you beg, borrow, or steal time? No, you cannot! You can't stop or start it, buy it, sell it, lease it, or rent it, and you certainly can't manage it...at least not in a literal sense.

The reality is that you cannot manage time...all you can do is spend it!

This led me to my second and equally important revelation: If you cannot manage time, then what can you manage? To get my business back on track, I asked myself: *How did I build my business and acquire clients when I started my career?* Looking back, it wasn't because of how well I managed my time; it was because I managed my activities well. What kind of activities? It was specifically my sales activities, like the number of sales and client service calls that I committed to making every day. Having clear activity goals and good daily habits was at the heart of what helped me grow my business.

Literally speaking, you cannot manage time. This is my second revelation:

You Can Only Manage Activity!

This is not just a play on words; it is a reality. As Mark Twain said, "The difference between the right word and almost the right word is like the difference between lightning and a lightning bug." Coincidentally, that quote came to mind as I was writing this particular chapter in the library off of the lobby in the Mark Twain Hotel in Peoria, Illinois, with Mark Twain's portrait hanging just above me.

You cannot manage time; you can only manage activity. Whether it's your physical activity at the health club, playing a sport or musical instrument, studying at college or medical school, performing the right sales activities, or any other activity you can imagine, what matters most is not how much time has passed, but what you do during that time.

At Best, Time Management...is a Misnomer.

This concept of not managing time but managing activity became the topic of some of my first motivational speeches. I can still remember holding up a placard to illustrate this point at a car dealership called Woodfield Ford in Schaumburg, Illinois, in the early-nineties (circa 1993). The dealership may be long gone, but the message is timeless and I still have a white piece of plastic about five inches high and eighteen inches wide with green letters on it that reads:

1957 - 2057

I introduced the concept while holding the old plastic sign at a Saturday morning sales meeting and said, "This represents my birth year. Since my goal is to follow George Burns' lead and live to be one hundred years old, this could be etched in my tombstone someday! Which part of this sign do you feel is the most important part?" After pausing to let people consider my question, I said, "Is it the year that I was born? Is it the year of my death? Or is it the time in between—the dash?

Arguably, they are all important. If it wasn't for the beginning year for any one of us, we would not have been born. That's when we came out crying and everyone else was happy. And, hopefully, when the final year arrives, the reverse happens. We will go out happy and others will be crying. But, the more important question is going to be: What did we do with the time in between? What did we do in the *dash*?"

What that dash represents isn't just the years that span the time; it's the time that spans the years and what you did with that time. The dash represents our activities and accomplishments during our lifetime, whether it's between years or hours worked. I would use the same analogy when I would hold up a sign reading "9 – 5" and ask, "What is most important, the time you start work, the time you leave work, or the time in between?" The same principle applies. *It's all about the dash.*

One of the best lessons about time that I have ever experienced happened many years later in Philadelphia, Pennsylvania, at my best friend's graduation from the MCP Hahnemann University Hospital. As my friend was exiting the stage after receiving his diploma, I commented to his classmate, "It's amazing to me how he can walk up on stage as Raj and walk off stage as Dr. Ambay! He could have chosen to stay where he was at or do something else for the last five years. He could have chosen to work an hourly job, yet he chose to spend time in medical school. Now he's a doctor, and his life is changed forever!"

His classmate turned to me and wisely replied, "Yes, *time* will pass anyway." More profound words were probably never spoken.

CHAPTER THREE

We Reap What We Sow

★ ★ ★ ★ ★ ★

You cannot manage time, only activity was the first piece of the puzzle and the rest of the pieces fell into place pretty quickly thereafter. Little did I know that the keys to turning around my business early in my career would lead me to one of the most empowering concepts in the world and be the same formula that I would have to turn to during my 50 Capitols trip!

When I thought back to how I built my business in the first place, I remembered that what made the greatest impact was making three sales calls and three service calls every day. That may not sound like much activity, but it fit my target market at the time during the pre-internet days and was done in person (not by phone). It also adds up…to 750 sales and 750 service calls annually, assuming you take off two weeks for vacation! If I was to rebuild my business, it made perfect sense that I had to go back to the basics of how I originally built it, by better managing my activities.

Why are activities so important? The answer to that is really quite simple: Dreaming about something alone doesn't produce results; it takes activity. Inspiring thoughts and goals may get the juices flowing enough to spark action, but without action, no result is possible.

Activities Produce Results!

The beauty of this concept is that it is very pragmatic and easily provable in any profession, sport, job, or task. Golf clubs do not swing themselves and neither does a tennis racket. It takes a mechanic to turn a wrench and a programmer to develop software; there will always be a direct correlation between activities and results. Managing that activity is vital and it's just as true in medicine, engineering, construction, and manufacturing as it is in painting, singing, flying, cooking, bridge building, and ship building.

Activities produce results. This applies as much in personal hygiene as it does to driving to work; it takes effort. Dreaming alone doesn't produce combed hair, clean teeth or transport you from home to work. Whether it's your hair brush, tooth brush, dental floss, or your car, they don't move by themselves. This truism applies from the time you open up your eyes and get out of bed in the morning, plant your feet on the ground, and take a shower, until the time your head hits the pillow each night. Even sleeping is an activity that achieves a result: restoration. As a friend of mine once said, "Success is simple, but it's not easy."

Activity is the key, but not just any activity; it has to be the right activity. These lessons and realizations were exciting and, initially, I thought that I had discovered an easy and pragmatic way to explain what leads to an outcome and how to better control results. At first, I thought that

I uncovered something new, but I soon realized that the concept had actually been around for years, even decades or perhaps centuries! What was even more surprising was that the answer had been right in my back yard all the time, practically under my feet and it could all be reduced to just *Five Little Words*:

We Reap . . . What We Sow!

The Law of the Farmer, as it is commonly known, conjures up a picture of a farm or maybe even a field of corn, along with the concepts of sowing seeds and reaping the harvest. This metaphor has frequently been touted and written about by many writers and philosophers over the years and it's the simplest way to encapsulate the concepts of time, activity, and results. The iconic Stephen Covey, one of the most prolific writers of our time, framed it up this way in his book, *First Things First*:

> *Can you imagine "cramming" on the farm? Can you imagine forgetting to plant in the spring, flaking out all summer, and hitting it hard in the fall – ripping the soil up, throwing in the seeds, watering, cultivating – and expecting to get a bountiful harvest? Cramming doesn't work in a natural system, like a farm... But in the long run, the Law of the Farm governs in all arenas of life.*

The concept of sowing and reaping may pre-date Biblical times, but it is very possible that the phrase "We reap what we sow" actually has its roots in the Bible. (Pun intended!) Unfortunately, there's just something about human beings that causes us to ignore the old and go seek the new and advanced. This may have something to do with how we are genetically programmed to grow, expand our knowledge, and seek new heights. This internal restlessness is a blessing, but in our continuous quest to improve things, we sometimes ignore the familiar and venture off to faraway lands to find the answer, when the best answers are often the simplest ones and also the closest to us.

There are countless references to sowing and reaping in the Bible like in 2 Corinthians 9:6, "He which soweth sparingly shall reap also sparingly; and he which soweth bountifully shall reap also bountifully." In Proverbs 22:8, we find "He that soweth iniquity shall reap vanity" and in James 3:18, "And the fruit of righteousness is sown in peace of them that make peace." The scripture that opened up my eyes the widest is also the most commonly referenced quote about sowing and reaping.

"Whatsoever a man soweth,
that shall he also reap."
GALATIANS 6:7 KJV

There is practically nothing to which the concept of "sowing and reaping" does not have some degree of relevance, including one's diet. I have certainly noticed that the worse my diet gets, the worse I *feel.* We've probably all felt that lethargic feeling after over-eating a big holiday meal with family. My weight is certainly directly proportional to quantity and quality of my food intake, whether I admit it or not.

While at Lake Geneva, Wisconsin, for a personal writing retreat at The Geneva Inn, I witnessed how this concept even applies to building a boat dock on a lake. Starting with the "crib" as they call it, which is essentially the foundation and blueprint of the dock with pre-formed, concrete footings and spaced holes, I watched from my perch on a balcony as a handful of men maneuvered the posts by boat and inserted them one-by-one. That was followed by placement of cross-members that went from post to post for support and formed the framework for the base. Then they laid down the white sets of pre-connected boards that formed the walkway and eventually the pier, complete with fifteen boat slips. The two-day process was a great visual metaphor of activity management in action and how activities truly produce results. I watched the dock being assembled as if it was an Erector Set® or a puzzle, piece-by-piece, action-by-action.

Whether you are talking about diet, construction, exercise, or about surgery, painting, writing or farming, it all comes back to sowing and reaping. It's a matter of cause and effect. Activities, whatever they may be, produce a result. Improve the activities and the results will follow. There is, however, one caveat. The payoffs from activity may not always come right away, but eventually they will. So, let's modify the old adage to say, "We reap what we sow…*eventually*." There is always a correlation between sowing and reaping. How well we sow is up to us and will ultimately determine what we reap, whether we admit it or not and whether we know it or not. Actually, it is a double-edged sword because while it explains why people succeed, it also explains why others fail.

This concept ultimately gives us all a road map for success, because if we don't like the results we are getting (reaping), we need only improve our activities (sowing) in either quantity or quality. It's where the Law of the Farmer meets the Law of Mathematics and is as certain as the Law of Gravity! The better the activities, the better the results. The only exceptions to this law are the things that are truly totally out of your control, like the weather, for example. For that and similar things, I like to refer to the Serenity Prayer authored in the 1930s by theologian Reinhold Niebuhr:

THE SERENITY PRAYER

God grant me the serenity to accept
the things I cannot change,
The courage to change the things that I can,
And the wisdom to know the difference.

Now that you've had some time to think about the common phrase, "You reap what you sow," consider how many times you've used the phrase yourself. Perhaps you've said it to one of your children as an "I told you so" moment. Let's not use it for shame, but instead, for personal motivation. Make it personal. When I was willing to reflect deeply and personally on this phrase, that is when I became truly motivated. The impact and ramifications of this phrase on our business and personal lives are much grander than anyone has ever estimated! These five little words can transform your life if you let them. My colleagues and I consider it the most empowering concept in the world!

I know that's a pretty tall claim and you might be wondering how these five little words can be so empowering? *They sound too simple!*

Well, by now, I think you agree that it is a simple matter of cause and effect: Sowing produces reaping as sure as activities produce results. Period. Try as I might to re-phrase it, there is just no better or more concise way of putting it than these five little words with just fifteen total letters between them.

Little refers to their size, not their impact. They literally empowered me to take control of the direction of my business and my life. I began to accept and reinforce that I was subject to (and accountable for) the consequences for what I did or failed to do. And as the second half of the phrase suggests, I was taking ownership and being proactively answerable for things within my power.

Perhaps even more importantly, these five little words gave me the freedom to dream and more importantly, put me in a position to achieve those dreams. This has been so life changing that I've written a little poem about it.

Five Little Words

We Reap What We Sow.

They have been known as the Law of the Farmer, yet they transcend every industry and every aspect of life. There will always be a direct correlation between what we sow and what we reap, eventually. Our actions will produce a result and if we improve our actions, the results will follow.

We Reap What We Sow.

Two of these words contain two letters, two have four letters and only one of these words has three letters. They may be just five little words containing just fifteen letters in total, but they are some of the most powerful words in the English dictionary.

We Reap What We Sow.

This matter of cause and effect is just as true in farming as it is in athletics, manufacturing, politics, painting, sculpting, drawing and building, as well as eating, breathing, sleeping, speaking, writing, and singing, as well as selling, teaching, policing, parenting, and coaching.

We Reap What We Sow.

All one needs do is truly internalize these words and your life can be transformed. These five little words are a pledge of responsibility and accountability, an acceptance that you are the maker and shaper of your own destiny, by your own actions.

You hold the key and have the potential to achieve great things, God willing, and become the best version of yourself! *We reap what we sow.*

Now, you have the same opportunity. Try saying these words of action out loud, except change "we" to "I": "I reap what I sow." It may be an age-old adage proven on the farms, but for us, it can be a pledge of responsibility and accountability, an acceptance that we make and shape outcomes by our actions. Since you control your activity and activities produce results, you have the power to achieve any result that you want!

How did that feel? Wasn't it a freeing feeling! By accepting responsibility for your actions and results, it will help you avoid the victim mentality that is so prevalent today and put you in control of the direction of your career and make your dreams possible. You may also find it inspiring to think of it in the context of your relationships with parents, siblings, spouses, co-workers, neighbors, and even complete strangers.

Here is another phrase that I have used over the years; a repeatable pledge that helps reinforce the entire concept:

RESPONSIBILITY PLEDGE

I am responsible for my actions and accountable for the results whatever they may be; today I pledge to do my best, help others, and optimize my time and activity.

We all have the potential to achieve great things! By themselves, those five little words are very empowering and inspiring, but the question that eluded me for years was *how* to ensure that I would spend my time wisely, efficiently, and effectively. That was a strategy that took years to uncover and formulate.

My hope is that by helping people embrace this concept in their career, it will transfer over to their personal lives and in the process, will make this world a better place. My other hope is that once you realize how these five little words can enrich your life personally and professionally, that you will share it with others to enrich their lives. I believe that educating others with this universal principle is a noble, providential endeavor and a great way to make a difference.

CHAPTER FOUR

The Magic of Habits

★ ★ ★ ★ ★ ★

It was somewhere while traveling through the New England states during my 50 Capitols in 50 Days trip that something hit me. It would determine the success or failure of the trip. I'm not sure if it was while driving along those beautiful roads in the northeast or if it came to me while I slept in the early days of the journey that many thought was unachievable. I realized that I had an "acre of diamonds" right underneath my feet, so to speak, that would be necessary to dig up if I was to be both disciplined and prepared to finish the trip successfully.

Let me first explain that expression or metaphor that grew in popularity after the writing of a book by the same name (circa 1890) by the founder of Temple University in Philadelphia, Russell Conwell. He is also well known as having founded a church and two hospitals in the City of Brotherly Love. Written before most of us were even born, "Acres of Diamonds" was also the name of a speech that Conwell was said to have delivered over six thousand times about an ancient Persian farmer by the name of Ali Hafed who sold his farm and exhausted all of his resources traveling the world in a search for diamonds. His treasure hunt was unsuccessful, and the impoverished and frustrated Hafed committed suicide before ever returning to his homeland. After he had taken his own life, however, the man who had purchased his property discovered that there were diamonds right in Hafed's own backyard! It is historically true that what was discovered was The Diamond Mine of Golconda, the most magnificent diamond-mine in all of history. (Source: *Acres of Diamonds*, by Russell H. Conwell)

My "Acre of Diamonds" was in the form of a strategy that I had used to build my business and recommended to clients for years. I was embarrassed to realize early in the 50 Capitols in 50 Days trip that I had gotten away from the very philosophies and habits that I had been preaching for years.

What seemed to be missing was a way to convert this empowering concept of sowing and reaping into an actual formula and strategy for success. I wanted to move it from something one says in hindsight to something that drives the plan. For years, I accepted responsibility for my actions, but how could I be more focused and disciplined with my actions to achieve those results I was dreaming about? True as this whole concept may be, I found myself focusing too much on the harvest. What could I do to ensure that I would do a better job of sowing, tending to the soil, and planting the seeds? Over years of personal trial and error as well as collaboration with my clients, I developed a set of best practices or habits that I was able to refine during my historical trip.

What are Habits? Habits are those wonderful things, actions, or activities that we do every day by reflex with little or no aforethought. Habit is a noun and is defined according to Merriam-Webster as "an acquired behavior pattern regularly followed until it has become almost involuntary." They are the habitual things we do without thinking about them, whether it has to do with personal hygiene or how you tie your shoe, or how you drive your car or how you perform at work.

Habits are especially vital in a career and so aptly described by Dr. Albert E. N. Gray in his famous "The Common Denominator of Success" speech at a Philadelphia insurance conference in 1940.

"The Common Denominator of Success is that... successful people form the habit of doing things that failures don't like to do."

Dr. Gray's quote about habits applies to any career and is just as true today as the day he wrote it. Some habits are good and some are bad; all habits are hard to break, though the bad ones seem to be harder. (If you want to identify your own, just ask your spouse or loved ones!)

In my case, there were five of them. They would be the final piece of the puzzle and a formula for achieving any goal...especially a big goal with a short deadline like the one that I was attempting! They were exactly what I needed to start using... ASAP...or I was going to fail!

As Aristotle said, "We are what we repeatedly do. Excellence, then, is not an act, but a habit."

Benjamin Franklin put it this way, "It is easier to prevent bad habits then to break them." Zig Ziglar said, "Motivation gets you going and habits get you there. A few of my other favorites are "We first make our habits and then our habits make us." by John Dryden, "Motivation is what gets you started. Habit is what keeps you going," by Jim Ryun, and by Vince Lombardi, "Winning is a habit. Unfortunately, so is losing." I am sure that they would all agree that there is tremendous magic in habits and ultimately, habits will determine your success.

Coeur d'Alene, Idaho, will forever be a special place to me. It is there that I realized that I must share my journey and the habits I clung to for survival at many times along my trip. I have refined them so they can be applied to virtually any goal in life, including those that may be on your bucket list. Living without regret sometimes means facing a challenge you aren't sure how you will accomplish!

All five habits appear in the order I envision them being used, though they do not have to be implemented in that exact order. At a minimum, they are interdependent and each one is necessary, to a degree, in order to achieve any goal, large or small. And I would venture to say that if you were to look back at any of the goals you have accomplished, you would find traces of each of them.

CHAPTER FIVE

Focus

Focus...On What You Want to Achieve and Why

The first habit is Focus. It brings to mind a Chicago man named Earl Nightingale who recorded a timeless message called "The Strangest Secret" which became the first Gold Record self-help audiotape that had ever been created, selling over a million copies. On it, this personal development pioneer and radio legend said that the great philosophers throughout the ages have disagreed with each other on many things, but there is one thing they have all consistently agreed upon: "We become what we think about." Nightingale likened a person without goals to a ship without a rudder, and that every time a ship leaves the harbor, the captain has a destination in mind.

That is why *focus* is so critically important. Ask any golfer, artist, surgeon, marksman, or archer. Having a clear focus on what you want to achieve is vital because as Earl Nightingale also said, "We move in the direction of our most dominant thoughts."

The value of having clear goals and steadfast focus became painfully obvious on the second day of the 50 Capitols trip! Equally important was the need to constantly focus on the reasons why I was doing the trip. Habit number one is: Focus on what you want to achieve and why you want to achieve it.

What I wanted to achieve on the trip was relatively easy to define, but extremely tough to accomplish. My goal was to visit 50 capitols in 50 days, but it wasn't just to visit each capital city or stand on the steps of all the state capitol buildings in our nation and drive away. My goal was to spend two hours at each capitol and be at every tour desk, on every floor, in every wing and every House and Senate Chamber, taking pictures of floors, ceilings, and walls of anything I could find that referenced God, Liberty and Abraham Lincoln. Recording myself, along with anyone who wanted to join me, reciting Lincoln's Gettysburg Address at each capitol building was also a big part of what I wanted to accomplish. This piece was added after brainstorming at length with a good friend of mine and fellow Lincoln aficionado, John Morris, at Eureka College (Eureka, Illinois) where Lincoln spoke in 1856. We were trying to think of a meaningful and unique thing that could be done at each capitol that would help spread Lincoln's message; he suggested the Gettysburg Address.

The idea of finding out how many references there were to God came to me when I was in the Illinois State Capitol for an insurance conference eighteen months before the 50 Capitols trip began. I decided to walk over to the tour desk to test a theory (and satisfy my curiosity) in case I ever went on this dream trip. I said to the two tour guides, "I know this may sound like a strange question, but can you tell me, Is God still in the capitol?" I knew they would be a bit startled by that question, but since I was wearing a suit and tie, I hoped they wouldn't think that I was totally crazy. Once I explained that I was looking for any physical references like the word God in a quote, a sign reading "In God We Trust," the presence of a Bible, or an inscription of the Ten Commandments, their reaction was even more surprising.

The two young men, both in their twenties, seemed embarrassed that they couldn't think of anything and remained hopeful that something would come to mind. Then they said, "We can't think of anything, but he might!" pointing to a more senior tour guide who walked up.

I won't forget the expression of disappointment by their colleague, Bob Remack, when he told me that there were only two references of God left in the capitol, which were in Room 212, the Old Supreme Court Room. "You'll find murals of Moses on the ceiling with the tablets and some cherubs on the wall" he said. Their reactions told me that I hit on something very important and that if I was to ever do this trip, I was going to ask that question and find out how many capitols in our country still had references to God somewhere in their building or on the grounds.

Taking pictures of references to Abraham Lincoln at all the capitols was a natural choice for me considering my great affinity for our 16th President. With an extensive collection of Lincoln pictures, books, memorabilia, and a conference room named after him, I have always admired his commitment, determination, and sacrifices in the name of freedom. He saved "this new nation, conceived in liberty," at its time of greatest crisis, from being broken up into a dozen squabbling autocracies. In my opinion, he personifies love of country. In addition, there was probably no president before or since who quoted scripture more than Lincoln did during his presidency. It goes without saying that I am a huge fan!

It was in South Carolina that I added to my list: Take pictures of any references to Liberty. It was here that a tour guide (Heyward Stuckey) showed us the bell displayed on their capitol campus, identical to the ones issued to every state in the country by U. S. Treasury Secretary John W. Snyder in 1950. They had the same dimension and tone as the original Liberty Bell that rang out our independence in Philadelphia in 1776 and were made by the same company in France, Pass and Stow. They were numbered and on them was a bronze plaque that read: "In standing before this symbol, you have the opportunity to dedicate yourself, as did our founding fathers, to the principles of the individual freedom for which our nation stands."

After learning about the bells, and realizing that I could not find any references to Lincoln south of New Jersey, I decided to seek them out at every capitol as well any other physical references that would symbolize that state's desire for liberty. I would find out that not all states have their Liberty Bell replica on display, but the love of liberty was ever present across all fifty!

There were also incremental goals that were dynamic and changed based on progress and experience. Added early in the trip was taking pictures of anything that showcases the state's history. This was sparked from seeing how proud everyone was of their state and hearing staff rattle off a litany of the things that made them unique, ranging from New Hampshire's rich deposits of granite and Delaware's "The First State" designation to New Mexico's unique round capitol at the highest elevation and Oklahoma's oil well in front of the capitol with a dome added ninety years after original construction. Speaking of domes, did you know that not all capitols have domes on top? On this trip I would count only thirty-nine capitol buildings with domes on top, if you include two that are officially museums. The remaining 11 had everything from cupolas to office towers pointing to the heavens. By the way, Ohio's capitol building, known as the "Ohio Statehouse" has the most references to Abraham Lincoln in it…and it is one with a cupola.

The second part of "Focus" is to know "why" you want to achieve your goal. For me, this evolved as the trip progressed. Waking up at the Hampton Inn in Rutland, Vermont, I knew that I was in trouble. It was only day two, and the reality of the first day hit me like the proverbial ton of bricks. I had almost killed myself driving in a rainstorm the night before…without windshield wipers! They worked, but they just didn't wipe…on the driver's side! I found myself sitting up to catch a small slit across the top of the windshield, or even more often, driving with my left hand while sitting in the middle of the car and aiming to the right of oncoming headlights!

Using my iPad that next morning in that Vermont hotel room, I recorded my first thoughts of the day about the previous day's adventures. I looked like a wounded soldier, but even worse, I felt like one. Then other questions flooded my head, which I wrote in my journal: "Is this trip really worth it? Should I continue? Can I make it all the way? Why am I doing this anyway? Is it really that important?" Here I was, on the second day of the trip, and I wanted to give up! My "why" was hazy and I asked myself, *Am I crazy?*

Under ideal circumstances, I could have made it all the way to Montpelier that first day—but life is not always ideal, and circumstances are not always predictable. A wrong turn and car problems had already taken me off schedule.

My "why" for the 50 Capitols trip shifted over time and yours might too, as you further clarify your goals and sense of purpose. Mine started out ten years earlier, strictly out of my extreme patriotism that took root early in life. I even thought about trying to bring my young daughter to all 50 capitols, but then she became a teenager and that dog wasn't going to hunt. From there, it morphed into a fairly partisan trip done before the presidential election and to remind people of Abraham Lincoln's political roots. That didn't feel quite right, so I decided to make it more of a unifying trip for love of country and in honor of Abraham Lincoln and our nation's veterans.

Why Lincoln?

Lincoln was our very first Republican president and has been called, "The Great Uniter." Since both political parties have embraced him and have laid claim to his legacy, I felt that he could be a unifying figure for the trip. This also has to do with why the Gettysburg Address was so central to the trip. I wanted to subtly encourage fellow Americans to embrace four of Lincoln's core values that he expressed that foggy day in Gettysburg, that of God, Liberty, Unity, and Patriotism, which Lincoln seemed to share with many of our nation's forefathers.

I also wanted to encourage everyone to re-read the Gettysburg Address, a timeless speech that was short enough to be put on the front of every newspaper in the world at the time and memorized by school children for generations. I figured that if it helped unite us once, it can do it again. Parts of the last sentence, especially, kept ringing in my ears during the trip, "We here highly resolve that these dead shall not have died in vain – that this nation, under God, shall have a new birth of freedom." It reminded me of our veterans' sacrifices in the name of freedom and became a great source of strength for me.

That sense of purpose was so strong that it fueled my mind, body, and spirit throughout the grueling journey when I felt lonely and wanted to quit. It was the reason why I got out of bed in the morning while maintaining an average of seven to eight hours and driving four hundred or more miles per day. This was a big achievement for someone at any age, let alone in their mid-fifties.

So, as you are clarifying your goals, develop the habit of getting focused by asking yourself, *What do I want to achieve and why do I want to achieve it*? Then, when it's time to execute, especially when times get tough and you want to throw in the towel, stay focused on the "what" and remind yourself constantly of your "why."

CHAPTER SIX

Plan

★ ★ ★ ★ ★ ★

Plan...How Are You Going to Get There?

Once you know what you want to achieve and why, then you need the second habit: *Plan. How are you going to get there?* This is such a crucial habit to form. Planning is something that comes easier to some than it does to others, and it's not one of my strengths. With some goals, you may be able to "wing it," while with others, especially the more complex, planning is absolutely vital to success. When it comes to travel, you better know before you leave which direction you want to go if you want any real chance of getting there! Though turning around or correcting course is always an option, you still need some type of plan.

The actual process of planning for my 50 Capitols in 50 Days trip started long before I left my home in Illinois. Initially, the goal was to start in Delaware and end in Hawaii...the first and last states to join the Union. But when I decided to do it in honor of Abraham Lincoln and our veterans, it seemed only fitting and proper to begin and end it in the two states that played such critical roles in his political life and legacy, Gettysburg, Pennsylvania and

Springfield, Illinois. When the tentative route was known, my staff helped by researching the hours of operation of each capitol building and preparing a great planning sheet that identified the driving miles between destinations, as well as the hours and minutes it would take between them. The exact sequence of capitols to be visited, though, was not finalized until the second half of the trip. You can see the map in the Appendix.

Then there was the mode of transportation. For such a lofty goal, I needed to have just the right vehicle that was reliable, comfortable, and properly equipped. Our 16th President was a primary inspiration for my trip, so it seemed prudent and appropriate that I should travel in a Lincoln. I chose a 1997 Lincoln Town Car to symbolize the man, the legend, and the legacy and purchased it just for the trip. Besides if a Lincoln Town Car was good enough for limousine drivers, it had to be a good choice for a long road trip! Not wanting to travel in the lap of luxury or invest too much, it was an older, less expensive model in the neutral color of beige to symbolize unity. This car was the perfect choice which was only further confirmed when I picked it up in Alabama and saw the license plate that read: God Bless America!

The idea of attempting to get to all the capitols in such a short time came to me three years before the trip was launched. There was something about visiting 50 State Capitols in 50 Days that sounded motivational from the first moment it entered my mind. It was also consistent with one of my favorite slogans: "Big Goals…Short Deadlines." I was surprised to learn that the domain name of www.50Capitolsin50Days.com was even available! Obtaining it gave the whole trip more impetus and reminded me of a quote by architect Daniel Burnham: "Make no little plans. They have no magic to stir man's blood." With a clear goal and a deadline, my dream was transformed and slowly came alive.

To get inside of all the capitol buildings in fifty days or less, and to do it driving alone most of the way would require a lot of planning! It had never been done alone before in this tight timeline. Though impressive, the closest trip that had been achieved, according to our research, was when two firemen did a fundraiser by visiting all of the capital cities. By the way, in case you didn't know or notice the subtle spelling difference yet, the location or city of our states' central hub of government is called a "capital" with an "a." The word that refers to the central building that houses the legislature, however, is spelled differently. Capitol buildings are spelled with an "o." If you did not know the difference between the two prior to reading this, you're not alone.

This trip became even more of a feat because our research indicated that only 24 capitol buildings were open on the weekends! (I thought 25 until I got there!) That may not seem like a big factor, but to do this trip in fifty calendar days, the need for intense planning and discipline became even more critical. If I arrived at a capitol building even minutes late on a Friday (which almost happened in Delaware, West Virginia and New Mexico), that would have forced me to either sit around all weekend until it opened or double-back, either of which could have caused me to fail in achieving my goal.

When it came to this part of the strategy, I also learned an important truth for all of us to remember. The bigger the goal, the more planning is necessary!

The plans that you make to achieve your goals may change after you start on your path to achieving them. That's okay! The most important thing is to have some initial plans in place and to be flexible along the way. Even commercial airline jets are off-course most of the time while en route to their destination depending on wind and other factors.

You may also want to set your goals and make your plans in reverse as professional golfers do. Whether it's Arnold Palmer, Jack Nicklaus, Fred Couples, or Davis Love III, you can bet that when they play a course on the Pro Golf Tour, they research each hole and where they want the ball to land on the green to set them up for a good putt. They plan the hole backwards and then play it forwards. By knowing where they want the ball to land in the fairway, they chose which club to use and so forth. So, if your next goal seems daunting, try to begin with the end in mind as you carve out your path to your goals.

Benjamin Franklin is credited with putting planning into perspective with his famous quote, "If you fail to plan, you are planning to fail!" You can be sure that successful professionals across all industries have learned this important habit: *Plan out how to get there.*

CHAPTER SEVEN

Execute

★ ★ ★ ★ ★ ★

Execute...On the Plan

As you read this section, you may already be assessing the first two habits (Focus and Plan) and where they fit into the goals you want to achieve. You may even be back-testing these best practices against goals you have achieved in the past to see if and how they apply. This leads us to the next habit that is critical to achieving your goal: *Execute...on the plan.*

Execution has to do with effectively managing your activity and it's a topic that I have become very passionate about personally and professionally. According to Merriam-Webster's Dictionary, "execute" is defined as, "to carry out, accomplish, perform, or do." It is about action, the way we *carry out* the plan, and *perform* or *do* the right activities, i.e. activity management. By its very nature, it demands progress. To execute well is arguably the most vital component that you can develop because you know what you want to achieve and why you want to achieve it. You have detailed plans on how to achieve them, but without execution or action, no goal can be reached! Dreaming about something alone doesn't make it happen. Yet with the right action, any goal or result can be achieved!

There are two things critical to successful execution of any sizable goal: the need for ample supplies of energy and discipline. You have to have the energy to perform at optimum levels physically, as well as mentally, and have the discipline needed to repeatedly execute on what is needed day after day, night after night, to see it through to the end.

Energy

In order to have sustainable energy, I knew that I had to get in better physical condition to help ensure that I was physically able to complete the trip. As my wife told me, "Honey, if you're going to do it, now is the time…you're not getting any younger." She was right, and at age fifty-five, I had to heed that advice and become more physically fit by improving both my exercise and diet regimen.

Since no one had ever done this particular trip alone before, there was no one to call on for specific preparation advice. However, there are plenty of people who have pushed themselves physically and mentally to achieve audacious goals. There were two people whom I respected for grueling physical achievements, and who were close enough for me to learn from. My nephew, Tim Straub, is an Iron Man competitor, and my friend, George Hood, is an ultra-athlete who broke the Guinness World Record for "Stationary Cycling" at age fifty and one for "Planking" seven years later. What I learned from watching these two men was the need for extensive training, planning, and determination to execute on the plan. When it came to my physical fitness, I needed to be equally disciplined with exercise and diet both before and during the trip. How well I did that, I knew, would dramatically impact my energy level and ultimately my performance.

My fitness training started four months before the launch of the trip and critical to my success was hiring a personal trainer. I found a friend and fan of the goal in Colleen Balla at our local Five Seasons Family Sports Club. She pushed me to get in shape. She not only trained me weekly, she also designed a fitness routine that I carried with me and could do while on the road. When it came to nutrition, I stocked my trunk with boxes of healthy food, like trail mix, fruit, nutrition bars, cases of water, etc. I even made my own fruit smoothies on many mornings, thanks to my portable blender! I would still drink an occasional Pepsi or hot chocolate for a caffeine boost, but I also drank an abundance of water and added the XS® Energy Drink thanks to a supply given to me by my good friend, Matt Baron. I am sure I could have spent even more time and energy determining my dietary and nutrition needs, but it all worked out.

Just as important as what I consumed was what I did not consume. I stayed away from junk food, candy bars, ice cream, heavy lunches or dinners, and avoided alcohol completely. I couldn't afford any time lost from lack of energy, either from crashing after a sugar high or from starting too late the next day. I even adjusted the timing of my meals to much earlier so my food would have a chance to metabolize and I would sleep more restfully. All of these plans and precautions dramatically improved my energy levels and were critical to successfully executing the plan.

Discipline

Discipline is also a key to success. As I mentioned in the introduction, I realized on the second day of the trip that I was not nearly disciplined enough to pull this off. If I didn't step it up, I would surely fail! This became especially apparent to me after realizing I made one HUGE mistake when it came to the execution of my plan. I had practiced what would happen at each capitol visit, but did NOT practice or plan for what would happen between them!

I formulated from my practice visits in Illinois, Utah, Indiana, and Massachusetts, what I was going to do "inside" each capitol and that it would take me about two hours from the time that I got out of the car to the time that I returned to it. What I failed to do, though, was practice what would happen between the capitol visits, with everything from posting to Facebook and making hotel reservations to journaling and following a daily/nightly hotel routine.

What I had to do between capitols and the pace that I would need to keep far exceeded anything that I anticipated. Having extreme discipline was critical! As business consultant and Catholic advocate Matthew Kelly wrote in his book *Rediscover Catholicism*, "Discipline is the faithful friend who will introduce you to your true self. Discipline is the worthy protector who will defend you from your lesser self. And discipline is the extraordinary mentor who will challenge you to become the-best-version-of-yourself and all God created you to be."

Once I realized that I needed to be extremely disciplined, the quest began for how I could develop it. Like the trip itself, this too was its own treasure hunt.

In order to execute, I had to be disciplined. In order to be disciplined, I needed to be focused and organized. In order to be focused and organized, I had to establish good habits. In order to establish good habits, I needed to develop daily routines and rituals. And in order to develop daily routines, I had to have consistent systems every step of the way...which all led me back to the very habits I needed to have in place in order to be successful.

Realizing quickly that the evenings were a good time to get some driving done, I didn't know how much energy I would have from day to day. I rarely knew what city I was going to sleep in until a half hour before I got there. My original plan was to have my assistant make hotel reservations for me in advance. Since that didn't work very well, I had to estimate which city I would be in or near around ten o'clock p.m. and call to make reservations from the road.

It was a work in progress that took me a week or so to iron out. The systems and daily routines didn't stop with making hotel reservations. The first thing I did upon arrival at each hotel parking lot was go to my trunk and pull out my duffle bag and the food I needed for the next day. You might chuckle, but even the placement of my clothes was the same every time, with the toiletry bag on the right and shoes on the left. I found the less I had to think about, the more energy I had to mentally prepare for the next task on my journey.

I can still picture myself walking into each hotel room and the routine that I used every time. Upon entering, the bag went on the bed and the toiletry bag on the bathroom sink counter. The hotel shampoo and soap were placed on the shower ledge and the towel thrown over the shower curtain. Even undergarments had their place and if my clothes were wrinkled, I would spray them with water and let them hang up all night so they would practically press themselves while I slept.

That same kind of discipline had to be used when it came to technology. After I was done creating photo albums on the iPad and posting a dozen or so pictures from each capitol visit onto Facebook each night, I backed up the pictures on an external hard drive. I also had numerous computer items which all had to be charged up daily: the iPad, the GoPro Camera, the Dell laptop, and the iPhone. They all got plugged in nightly.

Besides having a system for execution from the time that I walked into my hotel room until the time I checked out, here are some of the other daily routines I developed that proved to be very helpful.

- Walk the grounds and record myself reciting the Gettysburg Address before touring hours to get a head start whenever possible.

- Conduct my capitol tours in the same sequence, starting with the House then Senate, partially so I could identify each chamber correctly later in my notes and photos.

- Arrive at the hotel no later than ten o'clock p.m. and whenever possible, sleep in the capital city that I would be starting in the next day.
- Go to bed thinking of my next day's goal – not the ten o'clock news – and (hopefully) get six hours of sleep every night.
- Wake up every morning and journal my reflections on the day before for about a half hour. This was critical since I would never remember all the names and events without documentation.

I believe we all have the potential to achieve great things, if we do the right things and especially if we do the right things in the most optimal ways. The only way to do that is to establish good habits, stay focused, demonstrate superior discipline, and have great systems to execute. One only has to look at the structure most successful schools and churches utilize as a shining example of the impact these elements and rituals in general can have on living a purpose-filled life.

While reading the last few paragraphs, were you thinking of "how" you're going to execute your plans in the future? What about those routines you may need to put in place before you get started? If you ever feel like you're off track, don't be discouraged. That happens to everyone. Your habits and discipline will peak and wane as mine did. There's something about being human that makes that happen. Every once in a while, things get cluttered to a point of total disarray and you have to stop and regroup. You have to clean it up and get things back to where you started, organized and in its proper place. You don't have to look very far for some real-life examples, like your closet or even garage.

There will also be times that you want to stop executing, feeling tempted to quit. This happened to me even before the first day of my trip. I was crossing Interstate 80 when I was tempted to go west toward home instead of heading north on my planned route. It was in Annapolis that I felt lonely and homeless and thought about giving up. I was in Quantico, Virginia, at the chapel located on the grounds of the National Museum of the Marine Corps where I prayed for an hour to have the strength to continue. (In my journal, I called the chapel "one of the quietest places on earth.") It was in Denver that I felt paralyzed in bed and wanted to throw in the towel. It was during a visit home that I didn't want to leave. That morning, I wrote "When I woke up this morning, the fear factor or negative self-talk raised its ugly head: I didn't want to continue and questioned its purpose."

It is crucial times like those when you remind yourself of your "what" and your "why," and how they must be sufficiently strong enough to push yourself beyond your moment of weakness. They help you stay focused, dig deeper, and come a step closer to achieving your goal.

As I was writing this chapter, I was reminded that if I really want to accomplish the things that I dream about in life, that I have to take even better control of my diet and exercise habits and improve them! I must be more disciplined when it comes to my food quality, consumption, and timing, as well as my commitment to exercising. For if I want to accomplish my life's goals, I need the energy. If I am to have the energy, I need to eat better, sleep better, exercise more and minimize or eliminate alcohol altogether. These are not new to me, nor likely to you, since we all pretty much know what we need to do to be healthy. It just goes to demonstrate that sometimes the best way to learn something or to commit to something is to teach it. Actually, according to the William Glasser Institute, students retain 10 percent of what they read and only 20 percent of what they hear, but up to 95 percent of what they teach someone else. So, thank you for allowing me to help you. In the process, I've helped myself as well!

CHAPTER EIGHT

Measure

Measure...and Monitor Your Progress Daily and Weekly

Interdependent is a good way to describe the relationship between all of these habits. They are all truly dependent upon each other in one way or another and especially this one. Having measurable goals is vital to knowing whether or not we are accomplishing anything. Having metrics in place is also important in the planning stages and will always affect decisions while executing on your plan.

The habit or best practice of measuring and monitoring your progress might sound like a lot of work, even punitive, especially if you're not naturally inclined to this line of thinking. I know that I have found it challenging, especially the accountability that accompanies measurement. But fear not. Like any habit, it's easy to develop with the proper motivation and collaboration with others. Besides, chances are you wouldn't be the person you are today if you hadn't already been the beneficiary of this concept through progress measurement tests and quizzes through school, sports, or work.

You might not have liked the results, but they helped both you and your teacher or mentor make adjustments so you could reach for new heights and become the best possible version of yourself!

As a matter of fact, measuring and monitoring has to be done with virtually everything around you, not just with the food you eat. The roads you drive on were built with precise metrics, as was the building you may be sitting in at this very moment. There is no doubt that the cars we drive and the planes we fly were built using elaborate precision through extensive measurement and monitoring.

As you might guess, measurement is everything when it comes to travel and was vital in the 50 Capitols trip. Some metrics were more important than others. For example, one of my vital metric decisions was the amount of time spent at each capitol. The average miles per gallon and the price of fuel were important metrics, but not nearly as vital. From my practice runs, I was able to estimate the time needed at each capitol to be about two hours from the time that I parked the car and returned to it. That's about what it took to get through security and onto every floor and wing, visit the tour desk, Supreme Court room, House and Senate chambers, reserve time for unexpected but meaningful conversations, and finally, recite the Gettysburg Address!

I kept a close watch on the amount of time spent at each capitol building and wrapped things up quickly when the limit was nearing. It was all I could afford to spend at each capitol with any hopes of finishing the trip on time. It would come down to how well I executed the plan, after all.

Like the best practices themselves, some of the metrics were interdependent and were needed to calculate other statistics. The number of capitols visited per day was valuable by itself, but more importantly, it also helped me track my capitol pace. I recorded how many capitols were visited compared to the number of days that had passed. In the beginning of the trip I recorded in my journal how many days I was ahead of my pace. For example: "Day 2 (+2)." As I passed through Washington, D. C., our nation's capital, it was on the fifth day and I already had eleven capitols in my rear view mirror. I began posting my daily progress on Facebook for friends and family to follow along. By the time I passed through Florida, I posted "Capitol #16 / Day 9" and kept up that numbering sequence during the remainder of the trip for their benefit as well as mine.

This capitol pace statistic was tracked very closely because I realized that it was absolutely critical to get ahead, especially while I was in the Northeastern states. By the time that I got to Florida, I was seven capitols ahead of myself. My goal was to be ten capitols ahead before I crossed the Mississippi River so that I could have more time to cover the western states that were located so much farther apart. In addition, I wanted to have time to come home to visit my family every couple of weeks...so I had to get a few extra capitols behind me early in the trip.

I was able to fly home once and drive home once before crossing the Mississippi for the third and last time heading west. But the goal remained the same...to get ten capitols ahead of myself. Extra time also had to be banked to get to and from Hawaii and Alaska which would take at least two days each. The best I did on that goal was to be nine capitols ahead on two occasions: once going from Louisiana to Texas and the other when traveling from Indiana to Missouri and heading toward the Pacific Coast.

Another statistic of great interest for me to track was the number of hours of sleep I averaged per night. I knew that if I wanted to have the energy to complete the trip, and be safe while driving, I needed to have about six hours of slumber per night. That is also about the minimum amount of sleep that my body generally needs to stay alert and healthy.

There were so many other measurements that impacted my trip! Here are the highlights of some of the others.

- The hours of operation of each capitol building was an absolutely vital thing to measure and monitor on the trip. Few things affected my travel route or schedule more than when the capitols opened and closed as well as which ones were open on weekends.

- Every morning, I would dedicate thirty minutes to writing my reflections about the day before with as much detail as possible.

- Measuring the flying hours was also important, which I did from Sacramento, California, to the Hawaii state capitol in Honolulu, and from Seattle, Washington, to the Alaska state capitol in Juneau. I also flew home twice, once from Oklahoma City, Oklahoma, and once from Sacramento.

- Hotel costs. My goal was to limit my hotel room stays to one hundred dollars or less per night. When you stay in thirty-three hotel rooms as I did on this trip, it all adds up! Unfortunately, that wasn't always possible (and I splurged in Hawaii)...but I kept an eye on that measurement.

- There were many other things that were important to monitor throughout the trip: driving speed, items of clean clothing, calories, cell phone battery power, and miles per gallon in the Lincoln Town Car. After I was done, I made a list of trip statistics, many of which are interesting to review in hindsight.

Hours per capitol visit - 2-2.5

Average time driving per day = 7-7.5 hours

Miles driven per day = 400-450

Total miles driven = 14,900
[including commutes, side trips, and wrong turns]

Driving days = 35; Flying Days = 6; Non-travel Days = 3

Three-capitol days = 3

Two-capitol days = 11

For a complete list of trip statistics, see the Appendix
or visit www.50Capitolsin50Days.com.

Measurement has as much to do with the journey as it does with the destination, and it is just as true in traveling and sports as it is in setting and achieving your personal and business goals. You wouldn't go to a football game if they didn't keep score, would you? That was the question posed to me recently by a corporate executive to drive home how critical measuring effectiveness is to all organizations whether it's a company or a sports team. My colleague added, "Business leaders need to stop thinking emotionally. We should keep track of key metrics in order to make objective business decisions." Her metaphor may have been about business, but measurement is just as important with personal goals.

Measurement in sales is so important that it can be the difference between success or failure, mediocrity or excellence. When we researched data for one client, we realized that the difference between a new agent/advisor being retained in the business after their first year was less than one appointment per week! But how would they know if they didn't measure? Another startling statistic was that if a sales professional were to increase three metrics simultaneously (number of closing interviews per month from ten to twelve, their closing ratio from 50 to 60 percent, and their average commission from fifteen hundred to nineteen hundred dollars per sale) and kept that up all year, their annual income would increase by 82 percent!

One of my favorite things to say to sales colleagues is, "What gets measured tends to get done!" Insurance industry leader, Ed Deutschlander, drives this point home in his book, *Be the First Believer* as well as the value of measurement in general. Deutschlander writes, "If you have a goal and it is important to you, you have to measure it." He goes on to say that "If you measure it, you can manage it."

In many ways, all the metrics and statistics of the 50 Capitols in 50 Days trip were vital and could have greatly impacted the outcome. Having too many would have been distracting and confusing, so I focused on the ones mentioned, believing they were the ones that should be prioritized. I measured and monitored them daily, and as a result, adjusted decisions along the way. You may want to do the same as you are deciding what metrics you would like to track in order to achieve your goals.

This brings us to the final habit. Ironically, it was the first one that I turned to: Accept Responsibility...for all outcomes in your life. The 5th Habit is next; last, but not least. I decided that it not only deserved its own chapter, it should have a unique name.

CHAPTER NINE

The 5th Habit™

★ ★ ★ ★ ★ ★

In the last four chapters, you have heard about the techniques that were used to complete the 50 Capitols trip, but they are not just best practices, they are distinct habits that anyone can develop to achieve any goal. There are actually five of them and they all grew out of the concept of sowing and reaping, transforming it from an empowering concept to a strategy for success outlined step-by-step. Their synergy is unmistakable.

This last habit is so special and vital that it deserved a unique name. It can and often is used first and throughout the goal-achievement process, as it was in the 50 Capitols trip. It certainly helped me turn the corner.

The 5th Habit: Accept Responsibility... For All Outcomes in Your Life

This is the fifth and last habit which complements the other four and, suprisingly, I turned to it *first*. I couldn't blame my assistant for arriving late in Montpelier or my mechanic for my windshield wiper problems. I couldn't blame anyone other than myself for missing the turn just south of Lake George or driving into the middle of a torrential downpour. I couldn't blame anyone for my total exhaustion nor for my temptation to give up. I had to accept personal responsibility for being almost a half day behind schedule on the second day of the trip, for not testing my windshield wipers before the trip began, and for only practicing what would happen "inside" each capitol, not what I had to do "between" them.

I also had to admit that I had stopped using some good habits and established some pretty bad ones; I had fallen off track and didn't even know it! But like Zig Ziglar used to say, "We all need to do a check-up from the neck-up" once in a while. This was part of my wake-up call, and that it was! I had to take responsibility and start practicing what I had been preaching for years...or the trip would be doomed!

Webster's Dictionary defines "responsibility" as "to be called upon to answer for one's acts or decisions; to be answerable; to be able to fulfill one's obligations." I like to describe it as "taking ownership of and proactively being answerable for something within our power." Put another way, it's the ability and the will to respond.

What was especially embarrassing at the time was that I had been espousing about personal responsibility (and portions of the other habits) to clients, friends, and family for years, but I was not always following them myself. Responsibility is exactly what I had to accept...and luckily it happened on day two of the 50 Capitols Trip while in Vermont before I got too far behind! And as Winston Churchill famously stated, "The price of greatness is responsibility."

My sister, Ginny, once told me that "The day you take responsibility for all communication in your life is the day you are no longer a victim." That really opened up my eyes to the benefit of taking responsibility for how things are said, how they are received and, in general, my quality of communication with others. Shortly thereafter I realized that the same could be said when it comes to results in life. That's where the 5th habit had its beginnings and quotes from books that I read along the way kept reinforcing that outlook and philosophy. Here are a few of them:

Leadership consultant Maxwell Maltz said, "Times will change for the better when you change. You are not a victim of the circumstances around you, unless you allow yourself to be."

John Ortberg, author of *If You Want to Walk on Water, You've Got to Get Out of the Boat* wrote this: "The conviction that our effort makes a difference and that we are not victims of circumstance is what keeps us persisting in the face of setbacks. It saves us from apathy, hopelessness, and despair."

In his book called *Leadership*, former New York City Mayor Rudy Giuliani wrote, "A lot of leaders have catchy slogans on their desk; many believe in them. The two-word sign on my desk genuinely summarizes my whole philosophy: *I'm Responsible.* Nothing builds confidence in a leader more than a willingness to take responsibility for what happens during his watch." The acceptance of this philosophy across the police department was a contributing factor to a record decrease in violent and overall crime in NYC during the 1990s.

Coincidentally, while writing *BIG GOALS…Short Deadlines,* I met a preacher from Chicago, Pastor Mark Jobe, at our local Starbucks who had just written a book with a similar message. It is a book about Elijah in biblical times called *Unstuck.* In it, Pastor Jobe wrote, "One of the most common forms of distorted thinking is a victim mentality… Elijah had developed a bad case of victim thinking. You will inevitably stay stuck when you start believing that you are a victim and that you are not responsible for the cave you are stuck in."

As mentioned, I started with The 5th Habit first and you may want to do the same. By taking responsibility, it prevents you from the pain and helplessness of playing the victim and puts you in control of the direction of your business and your life, so it's a good habit to start and end with and useful while employing the other four. The 5th Habit can make a wonderful difference in your life and if shared, can do the same for others. Hopefully, you've already adopted it in your life and have developed aspects of the other four habits.

Perhaps it is only natural to take credit when things go well; credit is rarely shunned. But when things don't go well, it seems very few people admit, "It's my fault" and adopt Harry Truman's famous quote: "The buck stops here." I don't know why some people are reluctant to accept responsibility for all outcomes in life. I guess it's just easier to make excuses and point the finger away from themselves, rather than toward themselves.

"It's not my fault" many people say, it was someone else's fault because they failed to reach a sales goal, finish a project, follow through on something promised, or do something as simple as showing up on time. For them, it's always some outside force that led to their demise; they ran out of time, it's a bad product, their manager didn't help them, their grandmother died, the economy was bad, or it's the wrong time of year. And we all probably know someone who was late because of traffic or car trouble. It's either a natural tendency or a defense mechanism, or both.

Have you ever noticed that these kinds of things often keep happening to the same people? Do you know someone like that personally? Perhaps you are one of the many who consider yourself a victim of circumstance and have serious doubts that you are in the driver's seat as you go down the highways of life. Perhaps you feel like your life is out of your control, or that your success will be determined by someone other than yourself, by outside forces. Perhaps you feel more like a puppet than a puppeteer?

Everyone is entitled to their opinion. Whether you choose to take the credit or the blame is certainly your choice, and if that's the way you choose to live your life, that decision is an inside job. Regardless of where you are on that spectrum, we can all bear some refining and reminding. It is not for me to judge, but more wisdom of Earl Nightingale comes to mind when I think of this topic: "We are all self-made, but only the successful tend to admit it."

I will grant that there are some things that just happen and are out of our control which, I think, is why that bumper sticker *"Sh— Happens"* became popular years ago. I prefer to say, "Shifts Happen," which I think describes life more accurately. Good and bad things do happen. Change happens. Clearly some things are out of our control. To think otherwise is foolishness, and perhaps, blind optimism. Weather, gravity, equipment failure, and acts of nature are some things that are out of our control. For those particular moments, I like to refer back to the Serenity Prayer and more sage advice would be difficult to find: God grant me the serenity to accept the things that I cannot change; the courage to change the things that I can and the wisdom to know the difference.

The key is to have wisdom in knowing the difference and a willingness and conviction to act on it.

Anyone who has given up control of their lives to someone other than themselves, to any outside people or forces, is making a terrible mistake. If you have given up the dreams of your youth, if you've lost that sparkle in your eye or that confidence in your voice about your future, if you have lost your way, do not despair. So much is still in your control and within your reach! The hopes, dreams, ambitions that you once held onto can still be attained!

Look around you. Is there anyone achieving the goals you seek? You have just as much right and ability to that abundance, happiness, and fulfillment as anyone else, if you're willing to pay the price and do the right activities necessary to achieve those results. In the end, we are all the sum total of everything we've done and all the choices we've made right up until this moment in time whether or not we want to admit it. Consider these words written by James Allen in his book called, *As a Man Thinketh.*

> *"Of all the beautiful truths pertaining to the soul (which have been restored and brought to light in this age), none is more gladdening or fruitful of divine promise and confidence than this—that man is the master of thought, the molder of character, and the maker and shaper of condition, environment, and destiny."*

Born in England in 1864, Allen is a virtual unknown, but was probably one of the greatest writers of his time. This quote has had a dramatic impact on my life. A shorter quote that encourages personal responsibility is another one that is credited to Allen: "Circumstances don't make the man; they reveal him."

Admittedly, I have made plenty of mistakes in my life and have experienced my share of peaks and valleys, ups and downs, successes and failures. My performance has varied from tremendous to horrendous and during my lifetime, I have ranged from confident to fearful, competent to incompetent and from fit to fat, cash rich to cash poor.

For twenty-five years, I looked for a formula for success that would enable me to achieve any goal in life, obtain and maintain success, and help me do more and regret less. Well, there is such a formula and the 50 Capitols trip helped me refine the habits necessary, step-by-step.

Over the last several chapters, each habit has been outlined in great detail and as you may have noticed, the five little words, *We reap what we sow* applies to all of them.

Together, the 5 Habits of Success can help you achieve any goal in life or on your bucket list, even big goals with short deadlines! They not only help you clarify the "what" and the "why," they guide you on "how" to achieve your goals :

THE 5 HABITS OF SUCCESS™

- **FOCUS** ... on what you want to achieve and why
- **PLAN** ... out how to get there
- **EXECUTE** ... on the plan
- **MEASURE** ... and monitor your progress daily and weekly
- **ACCEPT RESPONSIBILITY** ... for all outcomes in your life

These habits don't have to be used in chronological order or in strict sequence. The 5th Habit is so vital to achieving your goals that I felt that it deserved a unique name. When you accept responsibility for **Focusing**, you get clearer on what you want to accomplish and why. When you accept responsibility for **Planning**, you'll do a better job on mapping out how to achieve your goals in incremental bites, perhaps even starting with the end in mind. When you accept responsibility for **Executing**, you take ownership of all of your actions, including those in your plan. When you accept responsibility for **Measuring** and monitoring your progress, you are able to gauge the effectiveness of your actions.

I used these five habits every day of the 50 Capitols trip, and I remind myself of them whenever attempting to achieve any goal, large or small. If you want to commit them to memory quickly, you may even want to start with memorizing them in this fashion:

Focus ★ Plan ★ Execute ★
Measure ★ Accept Responsibility

You may often find yourself jumping from one to the other to update and enhance them while on the path to achieving your goal, as I did. The most important thing is that each habit in some form is a part of your overall strategy for success.

These same principles helped our community launch a private effort and fundraiser to build an elementary school playground, order and receive the equipment, recruit volunteers, demolish, build, and dedicate a new playground on public school ground…all in just 49 days! And these same five habits were also used in my political campaign to win, against the odds, and be elected mayor of Burr Ridge, a suburb of Chicago.

You may want to customize the formula or tweak the title, but that's okay. This is America, the land of opportunity that grants you the freedom to pursue your dreams, choose your own path, and to do things your own way. You can even repurpose the title of "The 5 Habits…" to fit the situation or topic. I most frequently refer to them as "The 5 Habits of Success" but have also used them in different scenarios.

For example, The 5 Habits of Goal Achievement, The 5 Habits of Activity Management or The 5 Habits of Financial Planning, because the same steps apply. My hope is that elements of these five habits will help you achieve more and regret less in both your professional and personal lives; maybe they will even to help you achieve the American Dream! While there is no magic wand that guarantees success, lasting success can be achieved over time and with the right habits to sustain it.

Traces of The 5 Habits of Success can be found in many motivational speeches, goal setting books, and in the strategy of activity management itself. The power and impact of their fundamentals are undeniable and came to my rescue during the trip many thought was unachievable. I am pleased to tell you that this historic trip was actually completed in just 44 days! Though I did have some additional motivation at the end: to get home to see my daughter, Alysa, play in her final high school state championship for tennis.

The 50 Capitols trip was extremely humbling, challenging, eye-opening, and life changing. It was the most difficult thing that I have ever attempted and I wanted to quit countless times, but it was also the most rewarding accomplishment of my life. The capitols were beautiful, but the people were amazing, and the experiences and lessons that I learned on this trip were priceless.

It was a "dream come true" that an idea germinating for ten years would come to fruition and that the 50 Capitols in 50 Days trip was possible. What I didn't realize, though, was that the end of that journey would be the beginning of a new one and that the lessons would continue.

CHAPTER TEN

Faith & Friendship

★ ★ ★ ★ ★ ★

Starting in Gettysburg, Pennsylvania, outside the David Wills House where Abraham Lincoln finished writing the Gettysburg Address (and where he slept the night before he delivered it), the 50 Capitols in 50 Days trip ended in Springfield, Illinois, where Lincoln's political career began and in front of the Lincoln Tomb at Oakwood Cemetery with a Monsignor from the Springfield Diocese. Those two cities would bookend a patriotic pilgrimage that was both humbling and exhilarating. It was filled with unexplainable, serendipitous moments. To top it off, I completed the trip ahead of schedule!

The goal-setting strategy developed in our activity management business helped make this dream a reality, but there were two additional factors that were also vital to finishing this life-changing trip. Actually, what I am about to share with you is probably more important than anything mentioned in this book so far and critical to helping you achieve your personal, professional, or bucket-list goals. They are the same pillars that were critical during the trip and continue to prop me up to this day. They are faith and friendship.

The reliance on faith and friendship to accomplish this goal was underestimated. Admittedly, I never really factored them into the equation before the trip. The role of faith became fairly obvious early on, but the vital role of friendship didn't completely hit me until long after the trip was over. The trip could not have been accomplished without the help of all the friends who helped me along the way, not to mention the complete strangers who helped me at very key times! It was all part of my journey and personal awakening.

Clearly, I knew ahead of time that the trip was somehow, in some way, faith driven. To begin with, I needed faith in myself that I could actually complete this far-reaching feat. I needed faith in the plan that it could actually work. I also needed faith in the people around me who helped coordinate the launch. Above all, I needed faith in my purpose. My reason for going on the trip in the first place was for love of country and in honor of Abraham Lincoln and our veterans. This was what I was supposed to do and I felt that it was God's will. The fact that I was going to each state to answer the question "Is God still in the Capitol?" should have been one of my first clues.

A couple of years after the trip, I was reminded of God's role when I serendipitously decided to finish reading a book by Fred Sievert called *God Revealed*. This is a book that I started reading a dozen months earlier and in it, Sievert, former president of New York Life Insurance Company, talks at great length about how we ultimately have to wait until it is God's time. The reading of *God Revealed* turned out to be one of the finest examples of divine providence and it gave me the needed impetus to finish writing this book. It helped me realize how many times God was revealed during the 50 Capitols trip and encouraged me to share this part of the story with you. I should have better anticipated God's presence on this adventure. I prayed that God would watch over me and implored His help before the trip and in my farewell comments, but I totally underestimated His omnipotent presence and tremendous impact before, during, and after the trip. This just wasn't factored in.

The most common question I get from people: "Did you do this trip alone?" Without hesitation, I have proudly replied many times over, "Yes, I did, with the exception of two friends, Chris Faron and Dick Coan, who drove for about three days each, in addition to a couple of more days that Chris spent with me, getting me on track with technology and social media before taking a turn behind the wheel." Given enough time to further explain, I tell them how their help wasn't confirmed until after the trip began, but luckily it fell into place because I had no idea how desperately I would need their help. They basically rescued me. Their help opened my eyes to the role that both faith and friendship played in the trip and how providential moments like this made it all possible.

When writing the earlier chapters, I also started thinking about other staff and friends who helped out, too, like Jim Long and Sheri Lessig who did most of the planning and supported the trip from Burr Ridge. Then there was Eric Nerad and Dennis Batha from B&E Auto Repair who prepared the Lincoln Town Car for the trip. Friend and marketing/public relations guru, Matt Baron, also did considerable media outreaches at the beginning and end of the trip. Then, there were my friends and neighbors who put patriotic lawn signs at my home and the committee members and friends who joined me at the Veterans Memorial for the big send-off. I even had a police escort when I was leaving the village, thanks to the police chief. Though, I have often joked that I'm not sure why they seemed more excited to see me leave then when I returned!

Those shining examples of faith and friendship were all before I even left town. It continued from Gettysburg, Pennsylvania, where I was joined by my brother and sister, Joe and Jolly, and met Steve Sexton and Mayor Bill Troxell, and occurrences like that happened across virtually every state. And when I arrived at the final one, the Illinois State Capitol in Springfield, Illinois, I got choked up when I saw the entire state executive board of NAIFA Illinois (National Association of Insurance and Financial Advisors) had come to join me at the final capitol visit. I assumed it was coincidental that their statewide meeting was scheduled for that particular day, but I learned later from the state chapter president, John Wheeler, that they planned it that way so that he, Sara Decatoire, Lou Bufano, Bob Styrkowicz and Eric Ekstrom could join me. What a phenomenal example of how friendship and providence played important roles in the trip!

Also joining me at the last capitol was my dear wife, Charmaine, without whose love and support none of this would have been possible. When I saw and hugged her for the first time in several weeks, I broke down crying knowing the goal was accomplished and the long journey was over. Then, the NAIFA Illinois Board joined my wife and me, along with Jim Long and his wife (Kathleen) and daughter (Nora) who came down for the grand finale, in reciting the Gettysburg Address on the Illinois State Capitol steps with the dome and famous Lincoln statue in the background. Then it was off to the Lincoln Tomb to meet up with the monsignor who led us in final prayers.

Those are just a few more examples of the role that faith and friendship, albeit unknowingly, played during my trip. There were countless others who played a vital role and showed up providentially when needed most all across the country. Then there was the Abraham Lincoln factor which goes back to one of the main inspirations for the trip. Lincoln, showing his reliance upon our Creator, gave innumerable references to scripture throughout his presidency.

Entire books have been written on his Biblical quotes dating back to his campaign's "House Divided Speech" where he referenced Matthew, Mark, and Luke during the Lincoln-Douglas debates to make his point. Lincoln included "Under God" in the Gettysburg Address and had fourteen scriptural references in his second inaugural address alone. Another example was his Proclamation in 1863 to declare "The last Thursday of November as a day Thanksgiving and Praise to our beneficent Father who dwelleth in the Heavens." It was no coincidence that Abraham Lincoln, and his faith, played such a large role in this trip and metaphor for life.

The mere thought of logging all those miles again, over 14,000 miles in total, without a team of people to help, makes me shudder! But the fact of the matter is that I did have a team of people helping me at the beginning, at the end, and every step of the way. They may not have always been sharing the driving, but they were there in spirit, by phone (like my sister Jolly, who I spoke with almost every night) or during chance meetings at the capitols and at the frequent Starbucks, Subway restaurants, and the gas stations where I would stop along the way. Far more than coincidences, I even gave them a fitting nickname: Capitol Angels! They picked me up when I was down and pushed me forward when I wanted to stop. I don't even know all of their names, but I am forever grateful for their help and encouragement.

Without Faith & Friendship, Nothing of Value or Significance Can Be Achieved.

I was never really alone on the 50 Capitols trip and, as strange as it sounds, there were times when I was driving late at night that it felt like my hands were not on the wheel. I could only wonder where the bursts of energy came from, but I can guess. None of this could have been accomplished without faith and friendship, without the help of God and others, the people that would show up providentially when I needed them most.

My friend and neighbor, Kevin Kopp, said it best, "Mickey, you were looking for God in the capitols, but you found God everywhere!"

Yes, I did.

APPENDIX

Five Little Words

We Reap What We Sow.

They have been known as the Law of the Farmer, yet they transcend every industry and every aspect of life. There will always be a direct correlation between what we sow and what we reap, eventually. Our actions will produce a result and if we improve our actions, the results will follow.

We Reap What We Sow.

Two of these words contain 2 letters, two have 4 letters and only one of these words has 3 letters. They may be just five little words containing just 15 letters in total, but they are some of the most powerful words in the English dictionary.

We Reap What We Sow.

It is a matter of cause and effect and it is just as true in farming as it is in athletics, manufacturing, politics, painting, sculpting, drawing and building, as well as eating, breathing, sleeping, speaking, writing, and singing as well as selling, teaching, policing, parenting and coaching.

We Reap What We Sow.

All one need do is truly internalize these words and your life can be transformed. These Five Little Words are a pledge of responsibility and accountability, an acceptance that you are the maker and shaper of your own destiny by your own actions.

You hold the key and have the potential to achieve great things, God willing, and become the best version of yourself! We reap what we sow.

APPENDIX

50 Capitols Trip Map and Statistics

50 Capitols in 50 Days

For Love of Country, in Honor of Lincoln

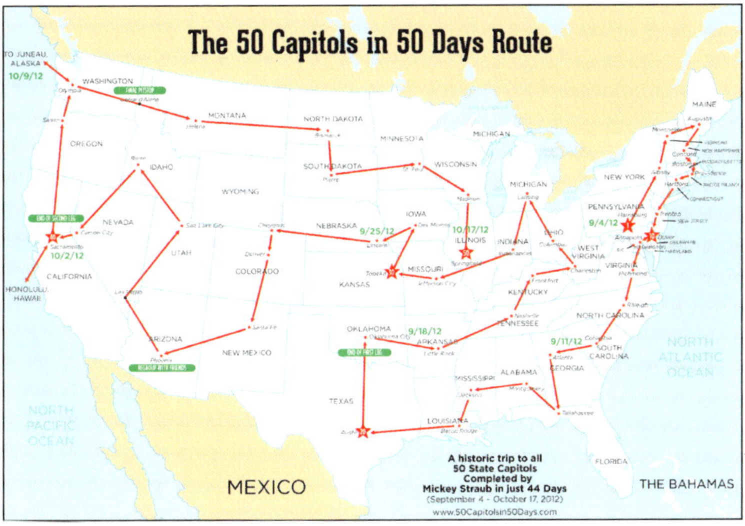

50 Capitols in 50 Days Trip Statistics

Capitol Statistics

Goal: 50 Capitols in 50 Days

Actual: 50 Capitols in 44 Days (Flew to HI and AK)

Inside Tours of Capitols: 48
(Tennessee was closed for construction; North Dakota not open on weekends during the fall.)

Time/Capitol: 2–2.5 hours

Miles Driven: 14,900
(includes commute, side trips, and wrong turns)

Hours Driven: 250–275
(approximately, includes side trips and stops for gas/food)

Flying Hours: 29
(includes HI, AK, and 2 round-trip flights to Chicago)

Sightings

God: 45

Liberty: 50

Lincoln: 27

Travel Statistics

Driving Days: 35

Flying Days: 6

Non-Travel Days: 3

Hours of Driving/day: 7–7.5

Miles of Driving/day: 400–450
(No driving on 9/8, 9/15–16 (OKC); 9/26–27 (HI); 9/29–30 (AK–flew back on 10/10, drove to ID); on 10/12 rested in Couer d'Alene

Approximately 630 Gallons of Gas and 43 Stops for Gas: MPG = 23.7

Lodging

Hotels: 33; **Friends**: 5; **Family**: 6

Sleep: 5–6 hours per night

APPENDIX

Gettysburg Address

by Abraham Lincoln

Four score and seven years ago our fathers brought forth on this continent a new nation, conceived in liberty, and dedicated to the proposition that all men are created equal.

Now we are engaged in a great civil war, testing whether that nation, or any nation so conceived and so dedicated, can long endure. We are met on a great battlefield of that war. We have come to dedicate a portion of that field, as a final resting place for those who here gave their lives that that nation might live. It is altogether fitting and proper that we should do this.

But, in a larger sense, we can not dedicate, we can not consecrate, we can not hallow this ground. The brave men, living and dead, who struggled here, have consecrated it, far above our poor power to add or detract. The world will little note, nor long remember what we say here, but it can never forget what they did here. It is for us the living, rather, to be dedicated here to the unfinished work which they who fought here have thus far so nobly advanced. It is rather for us to be here dedicated to the great task remaining before us—that from these honored dead we take increased devotion to that cause for which they gave the last full measure of devotion—that we here highly resolve that these dead shall not have died in vain—that this nation, under God, shall have a new birth of freedom—and that government of the people, by the people, for the people, shall not perish from the earth.

The Gettysburg Address is Abraham Lincoln's most famous speech. It was delivered during the Civil War on November 19, 1863, at the dedication of the Soldiers' National Cemetery in Gettysburg, Pennsylvania. It has been printed in countless publications and to this day is widely read, studied, and memorized.

APPENDIX

Thirty Times

★ ★ ★ ★ ★ ★

by Mickey Straub

"Four score and seven years ago..." Those six words and the ones that follow, echo in every American's memory. They are embedded in our culture and our psyche and roll off our tongues as if we were there to witness them being delivered the first time more than 150 years ago.

The Gettysburg Address was brief enough to fit on the front page of newspapers worldwide, helping it become one of the most famous speeches in history. Containing only 272 words and ten sentences, Abraham Lincoln delivered them in two minutes, in great contrast to the two-hour speech that preceded it.

For many reasons, it has become the most memorized in America, but it wasn't just because it was required in our schools for generations; it was because it was about the soldiers, unity, and a cause. Lincoln reminded us that "our fathers brought forth on this continent a new nation, conceived in liberty" and that we are a "nation under God."

He also re-committed us to the "unfinished work," that "these dead shall not have died in vain" and to "a new birth of freedom." The word "I" does not appear in the Address, but there are ten references to the word "we," three to "us," and two to "our;" and he used "nation" patriotically five times and acknowledged the soldiers ten more times.

Abraham Lincoln united us like in no other speech before or since by referring to everyone else but himself *Thirty Times*...and he saved the nation. The Gettysburg Address contained within it the formula for our country's future: God, Liberty, Unity, and Patriotism. May it unite us again!

This essay was written at the request of the Abraham Lincoln Presidential Library Foundation who asked Mickey to reflect on the Gettysburg Address using the same number of words contained within it: 272.

About the Author

The 50 Capitols in 50 Days journey was as unpredictable as the author's own life history. Michael C. "Mickey" Straub was born in Wilkes-Barre, Pennsylvania, and raised both there and in Kingston, just across the Susquehanna River. He was called Mickey (nicknamed after Mickey Mantle) even before he was brought home from the hospital. One of six children, his father, Albert J. Straub, was the son of an undertaker and his mother, Regina Kasaczun, was raised in the rectory of Holy Family Church in Sugarnotch, Pennsylvania, by her uncle, Father Francis D. Kasaczsun.

Mickey tried out for wrestling in high school, but gave it up to earn some money delivering newspapers at the age of fourteen, in part because he didn't like all the family arguments about the lack of money. Mickey actually started earning money even younger by working at a pool hall and playing competitively while in grade school. He credits his first boss and business owner, Joe Mantione (a former Marine) for ingraining his disciplined work habits and customer service skills at his first official job at Hess

Gas Station where he worked through high school and into the start of college.

Having five brothers and sisters (Ginny, Larry, Jimmer, Mary Jolly, and Joe) put him in a unique position to learn from the good and bad habits, the successes and mistakes of his older siblings. They also helped fuel his desire to become his best and were all great role models and heroes at one time or another. The spark to seek the secret to success started early. Reading inspirational, self-help books, success stories, and biographies became a life-long habit and his goal continues to be to read one book per month.

After graduating from his Catholic school education, Mickey attended Indiana University of Pennsylvania (IUP) located in Indiana, Pennsylvania, where he majored in Criminology, the career he wanted to pursue since childhood. He also had a minor in Political Science, his other strong interest. In addition to being the president of the 42nd Street Hustlers Intramural Sports Team and an undefeated pool player for four years, he was involved in Student Government and elected Senior Class President in 1979. Some of his most memorable college moments were the two times that he spoke with actor Jimmy Stewart in an effort to recruit him as their commencement speaker.

Mickey began his career working for the U.S. Department of State, as a clerk typist with the U. S. Department of Interior, Office of Surface Mining, Division of Inspection and Enforcement. Within months, he put his Criminology degree to greater use by transferring over as a Special Agent with the Defense Investigative Service (DIS), a division of the U.S. Department of Defense (DOD). There he graduated first in-class, receiving the Director's Award for Academic Excellence (Class 79-D).

His love of country and intense patriotism started to kindle while growing up in Pennsylvania and was further ignited whenever he visited Washington, D. C. and especially while working for the federal government within blocks of the White House. He felt honored and grateful to serve the country as a civilian, while working with many veterans both there and in Los Angeles, California. It helped to fuel his love for country. After a few years Mickey decided that working for the federal government would not to be a lifelong career and felt the free-market based private sector better fostered ambition and offered opportunity.

While still living in Los Angeles, Mickey went to work for the Ryan Insurance Group, a Chicago-based company working with automobile dealers that would eventually merge with Combined International and become the Aon Corporation. He was moved to Chicago to head up a joint project with Hertz Rental Cars, but that would be short-lived when the project came to a halt and he was transferred again and terminated shortly thereafter. For the next ten years, Mickey had a stellar career working for Western Diversified Insurance Group, a division of John Alden Insurance, winning numerous trips, awards and prizes and continually being one of the company's top performers.

In 1995, Mickey decided to give up his fourteen-year career to launch a company to make a difference across the insurance/financial services industry, and the sales profession at large. This was all done just one and a half months after their daughter was born, much to his wife's chagrin, but with her total support. Colleagues thought that he was crazy for voluntarily leaving a six-digit, practically part-time sales position, but he felt that's what he was supposed to do. Mickey wanted to make a difference and to better utilize his God-given talents.

Today, Mickey is founder and president of Sales Activity Management, Inc. (SAM), a unique company that provides custom business management tools, systems, and coaching services. Started from scratch to make a difference, today SAM helps 70,000 clients annually to build their business and achieve their goals. The company is still based upon the very Biblical principle, the one that helped him complete the 50 Capitols trip as well as develop the 5 Habits of Success. We reap what we sow.

Mickey also used this strategy for success to get elected in 2013 as Mayor of the Village of Burr Ridge, a Chicago suburb that is home for many business executives, entrepreneurs, doctors, lawyers, musicians, athletes, and coaches, as well as CNH Industrials (formerly International Harvester) and Mar's Chocolates Ice Cream division, where all the Dove, Snickers, Milky Way, and Twix ice cream for the country is produced.

On a personal note, Mickey grew up as a "Kennedy Democrat," but became a "Reagan Republican" after watching the transformation of the federal government and America from the inside when Ronald Reagan became President. This book, though, is not about politics, it is about unity, patriotism, and personal responsibility which is probably why one of Mickey's favorite quotes is by John F. Kennedy:

"Ask not what your country can do for you; ask what you can do for your country."

In addition to hoping to inspire you to set new goals, reach for new heights and check things off your bucket list, Mickey encourages you to visit your state's capitol building, to love this country more than ever, and to keep in mind Ohio's State Motto that is inscribed in bronze on the west side of their capitol building in Columbus: With God All Things Are Possible.

A WORD TO THE READER ABOUT THE COVER

for *BIG GOALS...Short Deadlines.* Like the 50 Capitols in 50 Days trip itself, nothing was done by accident, and some elements were clearly providential. The Capitol dome and Lincoln Town car on the cover are direct references to the trip. Since the trip and leadership insights were largely inspired by Abraham Lincoln, there are sixteen stars to symbolize our 16th President. The circle was chosen because of its strong resemblance to a target or bullseye, but shortly before this book went to print, someone pointed out that it also makes one think of the Presidential Seal. That is fitting since the trip was completed in just 44 days, the exact number of U. S. Presidents who have served at the time of the book's writing.